Medieval Castles

by Grace Hansen

Abdo
THE MIDDLE AGES
Kids

Abdo Kids Jumbo is an Imprint of Abdo Kids
abdobooks.com

abdobooks.com

Published by Abdo Kids, a division of ABDO, P.O. Box 398166, Minneapolis, Minnesota 55439.

Printed in the United States of America, North Mankato, Minnesota.

052025

092025

THIS BOOK CONTAINS RECYCLED MATERIALS

Photo Credits: AdobeStock, Alamy, Getty Images, Historic England Archive, Shutterstock

Production Contributors: Teddy Borth, Jennie Forsberg, Grace Hansen
Design Contributors: Candice Keimig, Pakou Moua

Library of Congress Control Number: 2024947609

Publisher's Cataloging-in-Publication Data

Names: Hansen, Grace, author.

Title: Medieval castles / by Grace Hansen

Description: Minneapolis, Minnesota : Abdo Kids, 2026 | Series: The Middle Ages | Includes online resources and index.

Identifiers: ISBN 9798384905295 (lib. bdg.) | ISBN 9798384905998 (ebook) | ISBN 9798384906346 (Read-to-me ebook)

Subjects: LCSH: Castles--Juvenile literature. | Architecture, Medieval--Juvenile literature. | Middle Ages--Juvenile literature. | Medieval history--Juvenile literature. | Dark Ages--Juvenile literature.

Classification: DDC 940.1--dc23

Table of Contents

The Middle Ages

The Middle Ages, or medieval period, was a time in European history. It lasted from about 500 to 1500 CE. Many castles were built during this time.

Europe
Asia
Africa

Medieval Castle Features

Medieval castles helped protect people and show power. It was common for a castle to have a **moat** surrounding it. The castle could only be reached using a drawbridge.

Atop the castle were **battlements** and arrow slits. These helped defenders of the castle fight from a safe position. Allures allowed them to move safely.

battlement
allure

A medieval castle had many rooms. There was a great hall for celebrations. There may have been a chapel for religious services. Prisoners were kept in a dungeon.

Famous Medieval Castles

Bran Castle's construction was complete in 1388. It sat in a helpful place. The castle was high enough to watch for enemies. It was also on an important **trade route**.

Europe
Romania

Alcazar Castle sits high atop a cliff in beautiful Segovia, Spain. A **fortress** has been on the site since at least the 1100s. Many royals have lived there over the centuries.

Europe
Spain

Dover Castle is in England. It looks over the English Channel. A **fortress** has protected the area since the beginning of the **Common Era**.

Europe
England

William the Conqueror, a **Norman**, took England by force in 1066. He became King William I of England. He helped improve the castle's defenses. In the 1180s, King Henry II built much of the stone castle seen today.

King William I

Tintagel Castle was built in the 1200s by Richard of Cornwall. Today, there are only ruins on the clifftop site. However, the castle is known as the birthplace of the **legend** of King Arthur.

Europe
England
N
E
S
W

Parts of a Castle

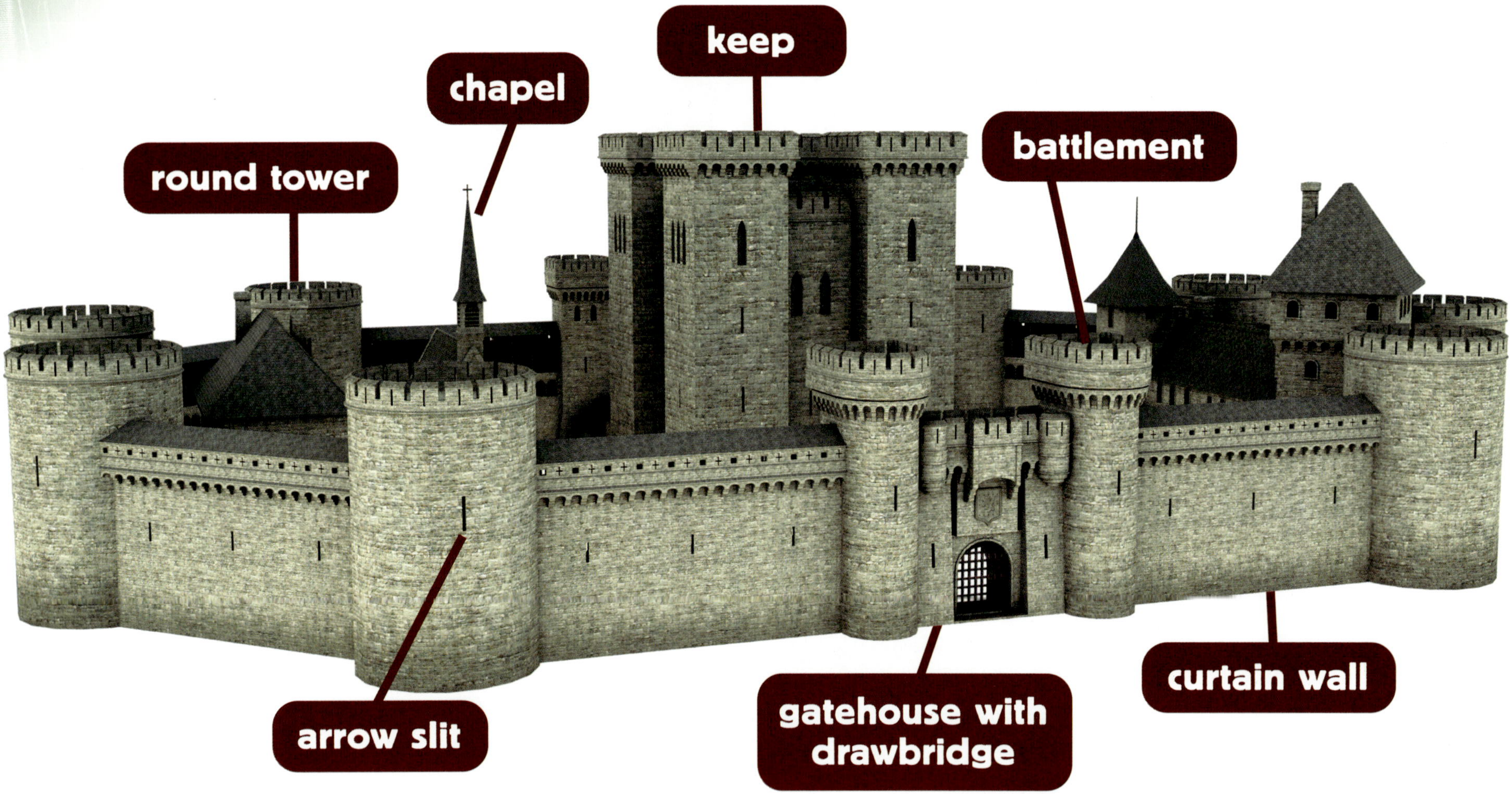

Glossary

battlement - a wall along the top of a castle that has openings for people to shoot through.

Common Era - the period dating from the year 1 CE. The Common Era is called "CE" for short.

fortress - a large, sturdy building or area, often around a town or settlement.

legend - a story or group of stories that have been handed down from a time long ago and that may or may not be true.

moat - a deep ditch dug around a castle, fortress, or town for protection against enemies. Moats are usually filled with water.

Norman - a member of a group of northern European people who settled in Normandy, France, in about 912 CE and became powerful in Europe in the 11th century.

trade route - a network of pathways and towns used to transport goods.

Index